Pocket Si__
Color For Calm

Adult Coloring Book

By Mindful Coloring Books

COLOR TEST PAGE

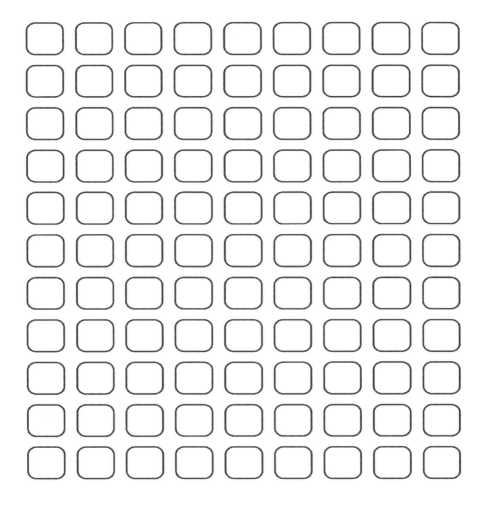

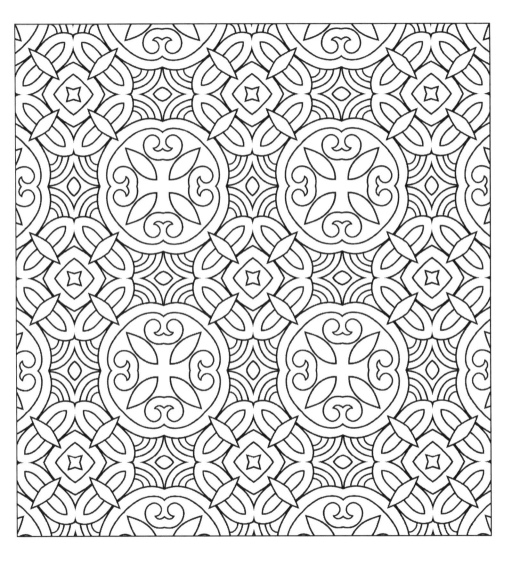

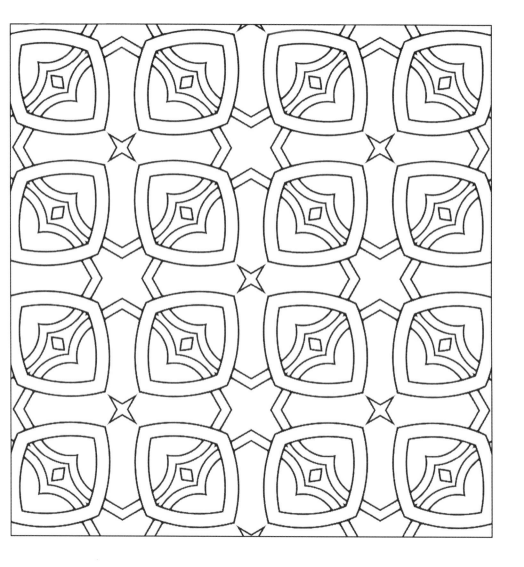

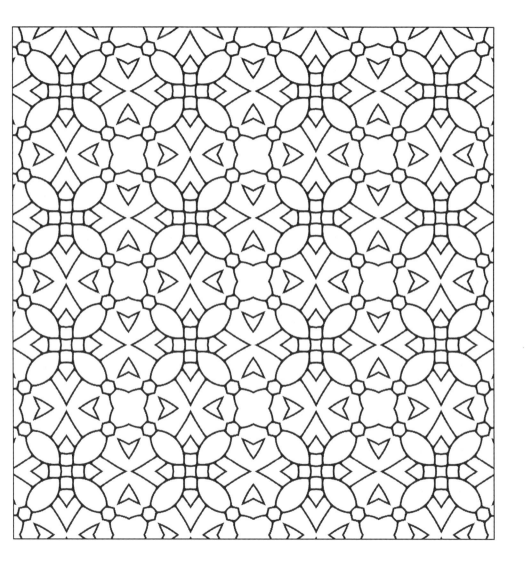

Leave us a review on Amazon!

Mindful Coloring Books:

Coloring books for adults
Coloring books for kids
Journals
Notebooks
Planners

Check out
Mindful Coloring Books

www.mindfulcoloringfun.com

amazon.com/author/mindfulcoloringbooks

Free coloring pages on our
Facebook page!

Printed in Great Britain
by Amazon

72741083R00041